FINISHING LINE PRESS

www.finishinglinepress.com

Naked Beside Fish

poems by

Yiskah Rosenfeld

Finishing Line Press
Georgetown, Kentucky

Naked Beside Fish

In memory of my mother, Beverly Rosenfeld,
who had a keen appreciation for art,
especially the nudes.

ACKNOWLEDGMENTS

With gratitude to the editors of the journals in which the following poems
appeared, some in earlier versions:

2River View: "Morning After Atonement"
The Bitter Oleander: "The Carnation that Defied Simile," "Legend of the
Nile," "Song of Songs," "Self Portrait in the Dark"
Glintmoon: "What Went on Without You"
The Ocotillo Review: "Poetry Submission Guidelines"
Schuylkill Journal of the Arts: "How an Artist Sees a Girl with Pomegranates"
Typishly Literary Magazine: "Paint Chips"
Voices Israel Anthology: "In Dreams and Chagall Paintings Everything is
You"

"The Carnation that Defied Simile" won the Reuben Rose Memorial Prize
and was nominated for a Pushcart Prize
"Poetry Submission Guidelines" was runner-up for the Julia Darling
Memorial Prize and won a Writer's Digest Prize.
"Song of Songs" and "Virtual Matisse Exhibit" were finalists for the Frances
Locke Memorial Prize.

Publisher: Leah Huete de Maines
Editor: Christen Kincaid
Cover Art: Susan Adamé
Author Photo: Cheshire Isaacs
Cover Design: Elizabeth Maines McCleavy

Order online: www.finishinglinepress.com
also available on amazon.com

Author inquiries and mail orders:
Finishing Line Press
PO Box 1626
Georgetown, Kentucky 40324
USA

Contents

Poetry Submission Guidelines

The white paintings were airports for the lights, shadows, and particles.
—John Cage, "On Robert Rauschenberg, Artist, and his Work"
(1961)

they should be the color of a loved one's shadow
painted on a clear sky at dusk
etched and chiseled from stone
each word a day's work
they should be students of blood and wind
before they graduate to paper
they should be edible
they should read themselves to each other at night
rub off when pressed page to page
run like a stampede of mice
a milk river between stanzas

they should envy our three-dimensional shapes
need us as much as we need them
let their corners grow wild
overgrown with white moss
silent reflections for lights and dust
as our mouths will one day be quieted
belonging to the damp earth
as they never belonged in us
they should unknot themselves
word by tangled word
and let us down
tenderly down
gently down
tenderly
in the
end

SELF REFLECTIONS

Self Portrait in the Dark

Teeth break in the mouth, jaw knotted and sealed shut.
Half black moons swim under the full moons of eyes.
Hard lines, hard lines: box the mouth, quote the forehead.
Bones under skin, gathered and sacked like garlic.

Really, there is nothing to see here.
Like a mathematical impossibility, this face
holds no solution. It will continue to haunt,
as if two were the wrong number of eyes.

Untitled 1954/55

Not the shock of unrestrained cacophonous
color exposed like the innards of an animal
still breathing, or the white walls cast in less
white lights, the whispered voices and a single bench.

Rather, how a home nested in their emptiness,
riotous spill-over adrift in cirrostratus space,
so exposed it was as if I had a right to be
there. No need to explain the pied eruption:

collaged letters and papers, soft pink scribbles,
surplus blocks of stacked wood on saturated orange
and blue prints, the yellow and black seepage
that are my daily risings-up and lyings-down.

For a moment I could lean myself
against the side of the walled room
and frame my life precisely as it is,
untitled, sloppily textured, still wet.

I let go the desire to feel desire or just to feel
that sets teens red-lining the secret diaries
of their thighs and stomachs with precise cuts,
twisting the knob right off Too Much.

A chilled bowl of summer pea soup
at the café across from Yerba Buena Gardens
drizzles from the spoon as if in bright green
conversation with Rauschenberg's *Untitled*, 1954/55.

I am not entwined on the grassy square with my lover
or riding a bike through the streets of San Francisco,
a messenger bag slung over my shoulder with a place to go.
It isn't that kind of painting. It isn't that kind of day.

After the laying on of hues, the stripping back,
the exquisite less that is somehow more, like the city
mirrored in a puddle slicked with oil, I visit the Calders,
remember two steel goats I'd pass under

on my way to the shuk in Jerusalem, yellow and angular
against a blue sky and graphite green olive branches.
I'd pass them again on the way back, bags full
of small, round eggplants, persimmons, lemons,

paprika, and a loaf of freshly baked bread,
one bag in each hand to balance
as I trudged the high grass beside the train tracks
until they ran too far ahead and out of sight.

Ciphers and Constellations

The spectacle of the sky overwhelms me. I'm overwhelmed when I
see, in an immense sky, the crescent of the moon, or the sun.
—Joan Miró

1

The summer of making do, morning dew
tastes like Frosted Flakes in a split wide box,
manna we scrape off the leaves

blessing the cool shade
before the sun sets it all on fire.
My child wants to believe

her teeth are wiggling.
She gets the whole world rocking
to prove it.

Even the weeds are scrawny,
leaned up against the fence
like bored kids outside the liquor store.

Whatever words might name
this crackling cement melt
under the sun's relentless heat.

2

Night is something else. Out of the tent to pee.
Alone in the dark meadow to dizzy down
under a clear sky teeming with stars

try to pin down what I'm witnessing
and fail, turn animal instead.
Let the sky just be its dazzling self.

Crescent moon. I see a listening ear.
Forest, I'm falling apart.
Trauma keeps reinventing itself.

My child sunk down in a sleeping bag
lined with pines, in a tent under pines.
Her dreams wax and wane.

Turns out tree therapy is just to go on being trees.
Being is enough.
I write it down on paper. *Tov.* I am good.

Big and little dippers ladle black soup back and forth.
Each star a solar system we can't see.
All the time we put into our little ones.

Not *very good, tov me'od*, like in the Torah
when humans were created, the sixth day.
Just fair to middling good.

3

Each child a sun we orbit, an intricate galaxy
of gravitational pull we only grasp a fraction of,
to the closest moon perhaps.

Words scrawl larger and larger,
the gaps growing bigger between them
like increasingly vast spaces between gas planets,

millions of galaxies—lenticular, elliptical, spiral—
spin like Spirographs,
swim me closer to sleep,

the last illegible scrawls
swirling and zigzagging the page
as bold and childlike as any Miró.

Later, I can just make out the words
alphabet train, measurements of failure, joy.
If even those.

‫י‬ The Letter Yod

Barbara's Studio, charcoal and chalk
Arad, Israel

What a comma looks like when there's nothing to separate,
a pause in an empty silence, more a mistake than anything.

Seeds float this way in the earth not knowing how far from
core or sky, birth or blossom. Babies float this way in the womb.

If there was a beginning to my life it's gone now. If there was an end,
it's gone, too. Or this is it, funneling up toward that sweeping curve,

brush-stroke widening into this now's end, in-
vitation to the next breath, next death, next breath, next ex-

hale. To be the snail inside this growing ocean of light, not
wanting to be anything but the snail or even the eye of the snail,

feet lost in sand, their ten *yods* dreaming of motion
a glint of sail where horizons where margins where words no

Legend of the Nile (Klee)

after an Ultrasound

On the edge of where my heart lies beats an ocean.
It glistens like the iris of an eye.
Having never seen itself, it makes no apologies.
It is stronger than death because unlike death, it returns.

Something strange and monstrous like a caged dog
keeps it hurtling against all shores,
as if trying to muscle open locked doors,
as if it could knead itself into a heavy dough.

I enter only at night on thin, brown boats of sleep,
those hand-drawn in medieval maps of Spain and Italy.
No maps. Only the knowledge that the world, like breath,
is round, that I will one day meet myself from the other side,

that the ocean is stronger than death and
unlike death, it returns.

Morning After Atonement

Noah's Studio, oil on canvas
Jerusalem, Israel

If not you, then at least
the ladders of light angling through your morning windows
voices still sleepwalking on the windowsills

at least the tall tilt of mirror
where liquid angels run up and down
the one place that you and I are both

at least myself as you could never see me
pregnant angel of your dreams
filtering through the rooms like the coffee and the light

If not you, then that angel's wing
rising to its elbow-perfect fold
and falling

THE GALLERY

Woman Ironing (Picasso) 1904

A woman is ironing; her shoulder
juts out like a mountain.
A blue fog pervades the room

defining shirts
starched to the white of an eye
the ambiguity of sheets and tablecloths.

Pressing the grass back down into the earth
she rolls out cities and continents—
the ball of the world stretched

to a thin plate. After,
what she holds in her hands
is the cool, flat handle of the sea.

Naked beside fish, I am two, I am one, a divided body in love with itself. Hip-heavy, one arm behind neck, a sturdy vase of a woman. All light flows up then falls in green daisied footprints. Summer with its blue heart enters the room, grapes of flowers cluster like hair around my head. Do you seek the pale flesh of my arms in all this color; do I fit like slick skin on orange fish?

Object of desire is an amalgamation of self and object—a melded creature emerges.

Buttons beaded up a new spine,
rising bone to the throat.
She speaks in spaces,
words not yet things
symmetrical, forgotten.
He speaks her back in rough lines,
ideas with bodies to show for them.
She emerges imperfect, loved: Antoinette in plumed hat, 1919.

The essential character of things is not one-dimensional, but two.

Room painted flat on a red wall: the shape of
things growing into themselves: chair, glass,
dresser, clock. Corners form by what chooses to
lean against them. The room arises in resistance,
to hold you up. The way a soul presses against
the angles and rise of the body. Without you, lost
objects   chair   vase   pencils   palette   float
in the red frame of memory, suspended, empty.

Despair and desire for lovers are caused by withholding.

Pierre, lay down the volume of things. Lay them down. The world need not weigh anything anymore. A seated painting watches like a ghost. It too weighs nothing. Then the green flight of music, larger than any metronome. Strive to be flat like this. The rounded essence rising to meet its surface. Curl, curl, curl of notes wrought into iron smoke. She watches cross-legged from the bottom left-hand corner. Part of you, she participates.

Frieda and Diego

How she resent him.
How she despises the clumsy
blue bulk of him.
Regal in jewel-necked beauty,
she places a small hand on his,
clutches the red shawl
and dips her brush.
Green skirts bell
round her tiny feet,
lighter than acorns,
her face a balled fist
of distaste.

Splayed out, his feet
are twenty of hers.
That's how small she is
when he is in the room,
though she dreams herself
larger than houses.
One day
under the soft swell
of her padded heels
she will crush him
to end this painted farce
once and for all.

Because of this,
her little smile.

How the Artist Sees a Girl With Pomegranates

She cups a pomegranate
soft in the brown boat of her palm
her long arms could encompass
the earth; they choose,

instead, one pomegranate,
one hand empty
a pale blue like sky encircled
by thumb and forefinger.

Three pomegranates, round and full
like breasts rest against flat planes
of green plate and over flat green hills,
two heavy fruits suspend in the background.

You choose to read invitation
in the sun-shaped face and wide eyes
the fat black curves of her braid tumbling
the plate of fruit angled to offer.

The pomegranates redden their fullness
spilling shadows on to your hands
empty now without them
as if they had been taken from you long ago

as a child perhaps and here they all are, offered
the blush and juice rising within you.
Still she remains
detached from the ripening world

like the two pomegranates still on the tree
or the boy you once were
before the pale blue cloth of innocence
was stripped away.

In Dreams and Chagall Paintings Everything is You

The lovers soar. Look and you'll find me
in back, an upside-down angel in white,
the one I love floating the opposite way,
his hands at my feet—is he catching
or dropping me?—while I clutch
the violin strings that sew his heart.

Angels are meant to fly, not dangle.
Why can't I ever get this right?
All I want is the right embrace,
his hand above my head, his other below,
mine resting on his pink elbow, together
looking in the same direction.

But now it's all mixed up: I'm third wheel
to a pair of slim yellow candles. Or am I
the fool, or that sad, blue cow? Look!
There's the farmhouse that emptied me out.
And there, some crumpled white flowers
like love letters never sent.

STILL LIFE

What Went on Without You

half-burnt toast and raspberry jam
showering in the artist's bathroom

reflection of stone fireplace in the window
my thighs that smooth, Miro-

inspired night of stars and moon
sharp pinecone

better suited to your hand than mine
coyote mint, not just the smell but the name

a silence that would have been a different kind
black ants, black ants, and the nectarine

Still Life of Lilies with Poet and Pine

for Li-Young Lee

How little they want of us,
the lilies and their watery stems,
how little they ask.

What would it be to slip inside
the still thrust of a pine tree
all those years of quiet unneeding?

I'm not talking about survival,
water and sunlight
fungi webbing the roots—

I mean the desire to be other
or to be
what others want,

I mean this very need
to be
what does not need.

Observe the lilies:
petals closed, petals open
easy surrender to the suitor of air

folding backwards
like broken umbrellas
in what we call dying

though a lily has no language for this
makes no comparisons
between life and death

or the poet beside it speaking
and sunlight squaring the windows
or itself and poet, itself and sun.

Beside the speaking poet,
lilies lie still in a glass;
through glass windows, pines

root the mountain,
the poet's words float like air and clouds
arms raised in branches

all the petals of my listening
unable to disguise
such longing.

The Carnation that Defied Simile

Writer's Studio
    Arad, Israel

The carnation on my table isn't like love
or sunrise
or blood on skin
or butterflies
or ruffles on a party dress.

For days now it has swayed out
of the sawed-off plastic bottle
next to the bamboo flute, photographs of some other life,
two rocks with moon shapes on them.

I want to understand how it feeds at my heart like this.
I have to know what it yearns for
and if I have wronged it somehow,
placing it here.

The carnation on my table isn't like angel's wings
or the tail of a rabbit
or a ringed moon
or olive wood shavings
or sleep.

To tell the truth, it's a bit
like thinly sliced radishes, pink edges
bleeding into translucent white petals.
That sharp, that raw, that open.

Mud Soup

Bay Area Discovery Museum, Sausalito

Mask over mouth mutes her pen.
What needs to be named on a day
so California calm it is barely of this world?

Cars on the bridge glide silently by, as do
wisped clouds, steelhead trout in the bay,
bubbles pushed through a sieve by the breeze.

Like drops of blood under a microscope, children
have spray-painted crimson watercolors
on a sheet tacked to the wall, spilled Kool-Aid.

What needs to be named? That xylophone wind
awakening the pines? The fog-veiled Golden Gate?
Wind, wake me, too. Unmask us both.

Lay my sinews and veins across a fluttering sheet
and call it art. Call it woman. Call it Yiskah.
Leave the body over there, on a bench, asleep.

Then who will call the wire cables
looming the bridge Strings on a Harp?
Who will call this child stirring mud soup

with tin ladles Hope? Or just Dirt-under-Nails Alive?
Who will ask if the bubbles rising past the red roofs
interrupt the sky or become one with it?

What would this day be without her gaze,
the geometric trestles crisscrossed under the bridge
just industrial steel without metaphor, the hills

at peace, soothed by the voices of children,
little hands clutching spoons and plastic crabs,
raking mallets over the backs of frogs?

If her questions float past the pines and disappear
will this, whether she names it or not, letting
the day nap cradled in salt and fog, be happy?

Urban Landscape as a Woman

string of bulbs, heavy black hardware, thin glass orbs where light will be.
parallel string of bulbs interrupted by square umbrellas.

how to crawl back into the womb of who she was before mother.
how to be herself and mother, the her inside the mother.

crisscross of lost and widening telephone lines.
wires that link or left dangling, a renter's line, gone nowhere.

where to find center when the city lists to the side as if she's a spoke.
how to be spoken, bespoke, speak, not need to.

two yellow round umbrellas set over wood picnic tables, twin suns.
thick drape of fog tinged the texture of baby's first food.

if her daughter's laugh at the top of the slide is or isn't hers.
red dabbed place in an oil painting where happiness resides.

past the last rooftops, sky torn from a notebook.
faintly lined, untouched by night's blue ink.

Song of Songs

I kissed the stars
with the kisses of my mouth

each ripe one
burst my tongue

fish wing eye arrow horn
a new language

of spark and shape
unscrolled on thick night

thousands of galaxies
spread like tea leaves

or spilled drops
of sweet wine—

light drips
from my limbs

the velvet truth
that we are nothing

the undressed truth
that we are all

the universe born
in the egg of my soul

where my heart
says yes

the Big Dipper of my heart
says yes—

you can touch it now
it will not close

you can pierce it now
it will not close

you can even
love it a little

it will not close.

GIFT SHOP

Paint Chips

A stack of paint chips in sandstone, lemon, and cream
spreads across the kitchen counter like a Tarot reading.
Paint the kitchen sandstone, and the house will sell.
Lemon, and our cupcakes will rise fluffy and light.
Cream and there will be sex on the countertops,
late night conversations at the table with two mouths
for each strawberry, more hope than our ravenous
appetites for eggrolls can satiate. This is how paint chips
will save us. Better than lottery tickets, better than cash.
The kitchen won't be so tired, propping its 60s self up
to groove to the olive green walls and brown tiles.
I won't be so tired, propping up the self I used to be
against too many near-expired cans of soup, crushed boxes
of unfinished Girl Scout cookies. The one dying plant.
The three 1/3 full liquid soap dispensers. All the teas.
But a fresh coat of lemon, a touch of cream on the cabinets,
sandstone to take my clown fall of a life seriously, these colors
whisper I could be someone, or better yet nobody,
the disappeared host of a dinner party. What no one tells you:
It isn't the color you choose. It's the act of dip and roll,
stretch of arms like you're waving to someone great.
Being worn out at the end of the day from hard work
and not from its lack. Still, what shade will it be?
Sandstone, lemon, or cream? I won't keep you in suspense.
You can touch my knee as you reach for the Cool Whip,
stay until morning, make Jackson Pollock designs
on the plates under sunny side up eggs on toast. Stay
longer if you want, until the sweet cream fades to ivory,
until we decide together on a new shade of blue.

NOTES:

Poetry Submission Guidelines

WHITE PAINTINGS (1951); paintings by Robert Rauschenberg [SFMOMA and MOMA]

John Cage, "On Robert Rauschenberg, Artist and His Work" in *Silence* [Wesleyan University Press, 1961]. The WHITE PAINTINGS inspired Cage's three movement composition for piano entitled 4'33", first performed in 1952. The piece is not silent, but rather is made up of "the absence of intended sounds."

Untitled 1954/55

UNTITLED (1954/55); painting by Robert Rauschenberg [SFMOMA]. Renamed COLLECTION for an exhibit in 1976. One of the first Combine paintings, which defy categorization as either traditional wall painting or sculpture.

GOAT FLAG (1987); sculpture by Yuval Rimon [Korenblum Garden, Jerusalem]

Ciphers and Constellations

CIPHERS AND CONSTELLATIONS IN LOVE WITH A WOMAN (1941); painting by Joan Miró [Art Institute of Chicago]

In the Genesis creation myth, each day is called *tov* (good) by the Divine. On the sixth day, this changes to *tov me'od* (very good). Genesis 1:31.

Legend of the Nile

LEGEND OF THE NILE (1937); painting by Paul Klee [Kunstmuseum, Bern, Switzerland]

Woman Ironing (1904)

WOMAN IRONING (1904); blue period painting by Pablo Picasso [Guggenheim, New York]

Virtual Matisse Exhibit

GOLDFISH AND SCULPTURE (1912), THE RED STUDIO (1911), THE PIANO LESSON (1916); paintings by Henri Matisse [MOMA] GIRL IN PLUMED HAT (1919); drawing by Henri Matisse [Art Institute of Chicago]. Toured under the title ANTOINETTE WEARING PLUMED HAT.

Frieda and Diego

FRIEDA AND DIEGO RIVERA (1931); painting by Frida Kahlo [SFMOMA]

In Dreams and Chagall Paintings Everything Is You

THE THREE CANDLES (1938-1940); painting by Marc Chagall [Private Collection]

How an Artist Sees a Girl With Pomegranates

GIRL WITH POMEGRANATES (1922); painting by Reuven Rubin [Private Collection]

What Went On Without You

The last line echoes "White ants, white ants and the little ribs" in "Snow" by Charles Wright; *Country Music: Selected Early Poems.*

Song of Songs

"Kiss me with the kisses of your mouth, for your love is better than wine." Song of Songs 1:2.

On the Gateways of the MERNEPTAH PALACE (13th c. BCE), ancient graffiti of a woman and child and, elsewhere, a fish were carved next to the hieroglyphs and drawings. [University of Pennsylvania Museum]

Additional Acknowledgments:

The poems in this collection celebrate a life-long fascination with the interplay between poetry and art. Arts collaborations and crossings have enlivened my poetic craft and my whole being. I am grateful to David Young, my advisor at Oberlin College, for planting the seeds. To disrupt my too-tidy poems, he instructed me to make quick notes on the backs of postcards. I had dozens of them from visiting museums here and abroad. A few scribbled phrases found their way into these poems. Years later, I experienced the joy of collaboration with visual artists through the Arad Arts Project, a gorgeous year-long interdisciplinary experiment that began in the Israeli desert. Some days I'd sit and write in the corners of artists' studios. Other days, I stared down the carnation on the writing desk in my apartment. I am grateful to the director, Nili Oz, and my fellow artists, especially the book artist and animal tracker Susan Barron, who herself had collaborated with John Cage. Later I served as poet-in-residence at the Brandeis Collegiate Institute in Simi Valley, California for another summer of collaboration. My gratitude lies with my students for their daring and creativity. I also want to thank my friend Lisa Wenzel for her close readings and encouragement, and my daughter Noam for her patience with this project. A special thanks to Susan Adamé for generously providing the beautiful cover art.

Yiskah Rosenfeld is the author of *Tasting Flight* (Madville Publishing, 2024), runner up for the Arthur Smith Prize and finalist for the Wheelbarrow Books Prize. She holds an MFA in literature and creative writing from Mills College. A Pushcart Prize nominee, awards include the Anna Davidson Rosenberg Award, the Reuben Rose Memorial Prize, and runner-up for the Jeff Marks Poetry Prize. Poems appear in *The Seattle Review, Lilith Magazine, The Bitter Oleander, December Magazine, Rattle, Wild Gods: An Anthology of Ecstatic Poetry,* and elsewhere. Yiskah taught poetry to youth in underserved communities as a San Francisco WritersCorps instructor and was an adjunct professor in literature at Temple University in Philadelphia. Her passion for collaboration with other artists led to poetry residencies at the Arad Arts Project in Israel and the Brandeis Collegiate Institute in Simi Valley, California. She currently balances solo parenting with teaching creative writing workshops around the San Francisco Bay Area.

www.yiskahrosenfeld.com

*9 7 9 8 8 8 8 3 8 5 0 2 9 *